A model of an Indian dye-mixing plant. The brass riveted gas-fired boiler and inverted vertical four-pillar, double-acting marine engine used to power the plant are believed to be apprentice pieces built about 1900. The boiler has fifteen fire tubes and is fitted with a steam whistle.

MODEL STEAM ENGINES

Bob Gordon

Shire Publications Ltd

CONTENTS

Published in 1999 by Shire Publications Ltd, Cromwell House, Church Street, Princes Risborough, Buckinghamshire HP27 9AA, UK. Website: www.shirebooks.co.uk Copyright © *1987 by Bob Gordon. First published 1987; reprinted 1999. Shire Album 207. ISBN 0 85263 906 6.*

Printed in Great Britain by CIT Printing Services Ltd, Press Buildings, Merlins Bridge, Haverfordwest, Pembrokeshire SA61 1XF.
British Library Cataloguing in Publication Data available.

COVER: *A pair of superb models of Savage engines mounted on a common boiler and built to a scale of one-tenth full size. The large one is of a number 6 centre engine which drove a fairground ride. The small number 4 engine was used to power the organ and its ancillaries. These models were built by Mrs Cherry Hill (née Hinds) and were awarded a gold medal at the 1985 Model Engineer Exhibition.*

ACKNOWLEDGEMENTS

The author is indebted to Jonathan Minns of the British Engineerium, and to Jack Mercer, President of the Tonbridge Model Engineering Society, for reading and commenting on the manuscript, and to Peter Mole for photographic work. He is also grateful for the helpful co-operation received from his son John Gordon, and from Argus Specialist Publications Ltd; Bassett-Lowke (SM) Ltd; Bassett-Lowke (Railways) Ltd; Miss O'Connor of Steam Age; Mr B. Carter; Christie, Manson and Woods Ltd; Brian Hetherington; the Mansell Collection Ltd; Mr James Sare; the Science Museum, London; Sotheby's Belgravia; and Stuart Turner Ltd. Illustrations on the following pages are reproduced by kind permission of: Argus Specialist Publications Ltd, pages 13, 15 (centre and bottom), 24; Bassett-Lowke Ltd, page 27; Desmond Beaton, page 6 (centre); British Engineerium (Jonathan Minns Collection), pages 2, 4, 5, 6 (top), 7, 9, 11 (left), 12 (upper), 14, 16 (left), 17 (lower left), 18, 19, 21; B. Carter, page 10 (upper); Christie, Manson and Woods Ltd, pages 20, 28; Clarksons of York, page 30; Dibbler Collection, pages 8, 16 (right), 17 (upper and lower right), 23; Ann Hatherill, page 32; Henley Engineering Publications, page 15; Brian Hetherington, page 10 (lower); lent to the Science Museum, London, by R. Hornsby and Sons, page 6 (bottom); Peter Mole, page 31; James Sare, pages 1, 22 (lower), 25 (lower); Science Museum (Crown Copyright), pages 3, 11 (right), 22 (upper); Sotheby's Belgravia, page 12 (lower); Steam Age, page 26; Stuart Turner, pages 15, 25, 29 (upper); Mike Wade, cover.

Although invented in the early 1800s, the more efficient and economical Uniflow engines were not developed commercially until 1908 because of initial problems. This splendid model of a Robey Uniflow engine, with its heavy flywheel for multi-wire rope drive, has drop-type inlet valves operated by eccentrics on a shaft turned by bevel gearing.

INTRODUCTION

There is something magical about model steam engines. They are fascinating pieces of industrial history in which shining brass, gleaming copper and burnished steel have been fashioned by craftsmen to epitomise the prototypes they represent.

We owe a tremendous debt of gratitude to all the early model makers for the devotion with which they applied their skills to the construction of magnificent miniature steam engines. These enthusiasts loved their work and with incred-ible dedication expended countless hours of labour in carrying it out.

Although much pain and frustration were involved, this was offset by the excitement of seeing their models take shape as they strove for perfection. The sheer pleasure they derived from doing work they enjoyed generated the creative energy which enabled them to achieve such high standards of modelling. Some of the enchanting results of their efforts are illustrated in this book.

OPPOSITE: *A handsome single-cylinder reversing horizontal engine model with over-mounted valve chest, built by Robson in 1886. Horizontal engines first appeared in 1801, but it was thought that excessive cylinder wear would occur and they did not come into general use until the second half of the nineteenth century. Huge machines with multi-wire rope drives were then installed in mills and factories.*

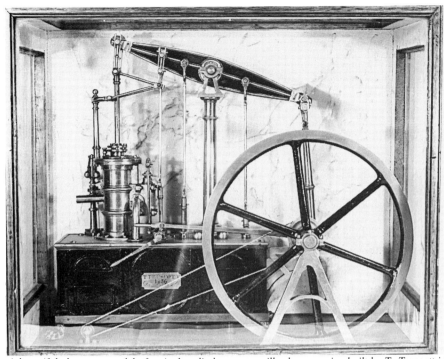

A beautiful glass-case model of a single-cylinder, centre-pillar beam engine built by T. Truscott in 1836. The flywheel is supported by an A-frame and the cast iron base by claw feet.

STEAM ENGINES

Following the invention by the Marquis of Worcester of a steam device for raising water, in 1663, notable contributions were made to the development of steam engines by Savery, Newcomen, Watt and many others. Some of the earliest engines were very crude and were often built into engine room walls. Later engines became more decorative and many reflected the Victorian genius for artistically ornate yet functional craftsmanship; Egyptian-style lotus-headed columns, fluted Doric columns and Corinthian and Gothic styles were among those introduced. Beam engines with these classical stylings make very attractive models.

Model steam engines fall into seven categories: development or experimental models; those made to support patent applications; models used as visual aids for publicity and sales purposes; exhibi-

tion models such as those made for the Great Exhibition of 1851 and for museums; apprentice pieces made by apprentices as part of their training; amateur 'scratch built' models (many of which were made just for the sheer creative joy of doing so); and commercial models supplied complete or made from sets of castings and parts.

Ranging from slow-working eighteenth-century beam engines to the high-speed engines and turbines of the twentieth century, many different types of steam engines were developed. As models they can be divided into two groups: showcase or display models and working models. Static models intended for display purposes only are often made without having the means of raising steam. If required to become operational at a later date they can be worked by compressed

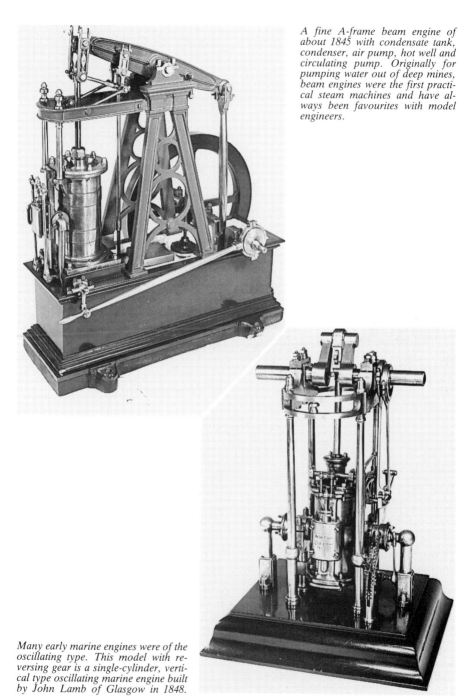

A fine A-frame beam engine of about 1845 with condensate tank, condenser, air pump, hot well and circulating pump. Originally for pumping water out of deep mines, beam engines were the first practical steam machines and have always been favourites with model engineers.

Many early marine engines were of the oscillating type. This model with reversing gear is a single-cylinder, vertical type oscillating marine engine built by John Lamb of Glasgow in 1848.

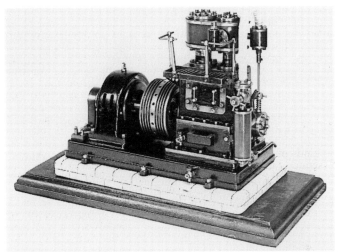

In the 1880s, when slow-speed engines were first used in the electricity supply industry, large flywheels and long belt drives were necessary to obtain the high generator speeds required. A demand therefore arose for high-speed direct-coupled engines. This is a model of an early twentieth-century prototype generating set.

RIGHT: *The construction of a simple oscillating-cylinder marine-type engine of this kind will enable the novice to get a feel for model engineering.*

BELOW: *This beautifully proportioned model of a Hornsby horizontal engine of 1885 has a disc crank, speed governor and wood-lagged cylinder.*

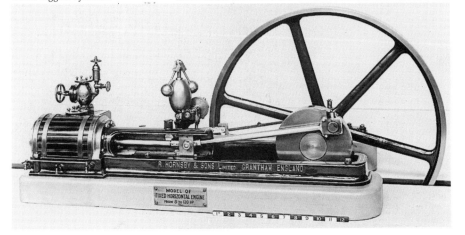

air or electricity. These models can be made strictly to scale and fully detailed. Working models intended for operation by live steam are usually supplied complete with boilers but are sometimes provided with steam from a central source. As far as is practicable working models are also built to scale, but sometimes unnecessary detail is omitted and scale accuracy has to be tempered with modifications in design to ensure satisfactory operation.

There are also three kinds of models: freelance, scale and scratch built. A freelance model is one which is not based upon any particular prototype and is not necessarily built to scale. Scale models are built to a definite scale in relation to their prototypes. Models which are usually made to scale, but in which ready-made parts are not used, are called scratch built.

When purchasing a model steam engine, either for live steam operation or to add to a static collection, it is important to be able to recognise a good one. To assess the real quality of a model the following questions need to be answered. Is it an accurate replica of the prototype it represents? Is it accurate to scale? Are the materials and methods of construction authentic to the prototype? Is the model well finished? How much attention has been paid to detail? Is the model a 'one off' built from scratch, or has it been made from mass-produced castings and parts? Is the model complete? Does the boiler carry a test certificate? Another factor which sometimes has to be taken into consideration is the novelty value of the model.

Although age is in itself not so important with model steam engines as with the toy type, rare models are always much sought after, especially those with historical associations. The assessment of a good model is, therefore, a matter of professional judgement and includes many factors which the layman would have difficulty in evaluating.

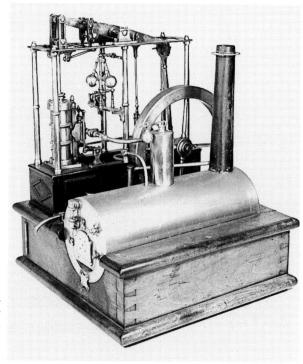

A single-cylinder, six-pillar beam engine with brass boiler and weight-type safety valve. Mounted on a wooden box base, this is a working demonstration model of about 1835.

7

A Stuart Turner beam engine which is not a scale model of any particular prototype. Because it moves slowly it requires only a small spirit-fired boiler and, being fitted with Watt's parallel motion, is a fascinating model to watch when working. When this photograph was taken the displacement lubricator had not been fitted.

HOW A STEAM ENGINE WORKS

Water contains latent energy which can be released by boiling it and converting it to steam. If heated in an open container water boils at 100 C (212 F), and 568 ml (1 pint) of water will boil into 933 litres (1642 pints) of steam. As this expansive force of steam can escape freely to the atmosphere it merely counter-balances the atmospheric pressure of 1.03 kg/sq cm (14.71 pounds per square inch [psi]), which is marked as 0 psi on a steam pressure gauge. No additional pressure will be built up to perform any useful work.

However, if steam is generated in an enclosed boiler from which it cannot escape, its pressure can be increased far above that of the atmosphere by applying heat in excess of the normal boiling point of 100 C. As the generation of steam increases it exerts pressure on the boiler and the surface of the water within it,

retards the formation of steam bubbles and causes the temperature of the water to rise. The steam, being elastic, becomes compressed and decreases in volume as its temperature and pressure increase. More and more heat is then required to produce additional steam, and it is the powerfully expansive force of this steam, when released under pressure from the boiler, which is used to drive steam engines.

As the steam is piped to a steam engine it expands and flows under pressure to the cylinder, a hollow metal tube inside which is a metal plunger called a piston. This has a rod attached to one end. In the case of a beam engine the other end of the rod is connected to one end of the beam either by a chain or by the 'parallel motion'. With an *atmospheric beam pumping engine*, when the piston is at the top of its stroke steam is admitted below

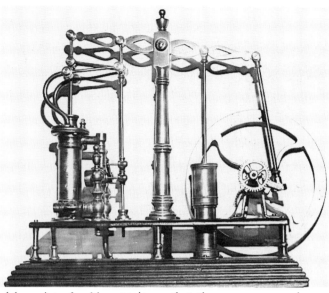

An early nineteenth-century, centre-pillar model beam engine with decorative fretted beam, rod-driven, plug-valve gear and water pump.

it and then condensed by a jet of cold water. This creates a vacuum and allows the piston to be pushed down again by the pressure of the atmosphere, pulling the beam with it. Steam is again admitted below the piston at a pressure sufficient to balance the atmospheric pressure, and the over-balancing weight of the beam and pump rods then pulls the piston up again so that the sequence can be repeated.

In a *single-acting non-atmospheric beam engine* the piston is pushed down by low-pressure steam and the weight of the beam pulls it up again. With a *double-acting engine* the piston is pushed up and down by steam. However, as the piston rod moves in a straight path, whereas the

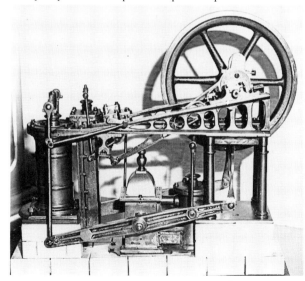

A rare and unusual model of an early nineteenth-century side-lever beam engine fitted with condenser and air pump. With low mounted beams, engines of this kind were used for some of the early paddle-steamers where head room and a low centre of gravity were critical. After 1850 the inverted vertical triple-expansion engine came into general use for marine work.

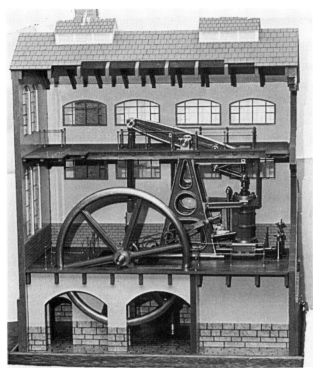

LEFT: *A model of a non-condensing beam engine with cast A-frames based on eighteenth-century practice. It was built by Mr B. Carter from constructional details published in the 'Model Engineer' in the 1950s.*

BELOW: *A model of a horizontal mill engine with disc crank, slide bars and wood-lagged cylinder, mounted on a brass table and wooden base.*

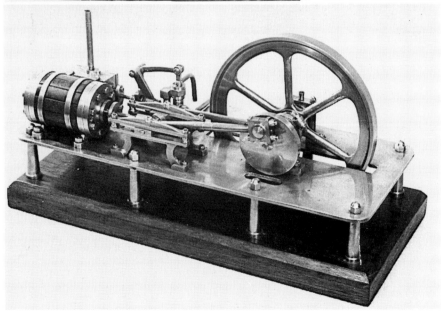

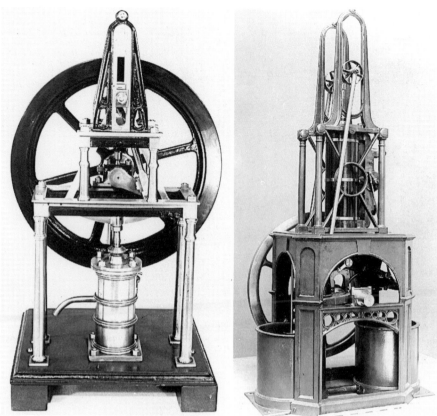

LEFT: *A four-pillar, single-cylinder steeple engine in which the cylinder is located beneath the crankshaft, the piston rod being connected to the crosshead by two long connecting rods. This was modelled on a prototype made in Westmorland in 1820.*
RIGHT: *A fine model, of about 1815, of Maudslay's table engine with a vertical cylinder lagged with wood. The crankshaft below the table was driven by return connecting rods.*

end of the beam moves in a circular one, the piston rod is linked to one end of the beam by an ingenious arrangement of pivoted levers and links known as 'Watt's parallel motion'. This keeps the piston and its rod moving in a straight line.

To enable steam power to be used for purposes other than the original one of pumping water, it was necessary to convert the up-and-down motion of the rocking beam into rotary motion. The most successful way of doing this was with a crank patented by James Pickard in 1780.

With *alternative reciprocating engines* the piston rods are coupled to the little ends of the connecting rods, the big ends of which directly turn the crankshafts, thereby converting the to-and-fro motion of the pistons into rotary motion. The piston rods are guided by crossheads, and steam is admitted to and exhausted from the cylinders on each stroke of the engines, usually by slide or piston valves operated from eccentric sheaves on the crankshafts. The amount by which the eccentrics are out of centre is designed to give the desired travel to the valves. The steam acts expansively and continues to drive the pistons to the end of their strokes even after the steam inlets are closed.

11

A fine French single-cylinder horizontal model mill engine with curved spoke flywheel, built by Frot in 1945. It is fitted with flywheel barring gear, ball-weight governor, drip-feed lubricators and a continental cylinder oil pump.

The constant speeds required for driving machines were obtained, except with large marine engines, by attaching heavy flywheels to the crankshafts. These stored up kinetic energy when turning and released it again when no steam pressure was being applied at the end of each stroke, or when a load was suddenly applied, thus smoothing out any erratic movement. The speed was controlled by 'governors' which kept the flywheels rotating more or less uniformly irrespective of fluctuations in steam pressure or applied loads.

Even after leaving the cylinders of steam engines the steam still contains expansive energy. To harness this, *compound engines* were invented in 1776 in

Compounding uses the expansive properties of steam up to four times in high, intermediate and low pressure cylinders of increasing diameters. This Stuart Turner model is a triple-expansion compound marine engine of about 1950. Large flywheels are not fitted to marine engines because, in rough seas, gyroscopic effects would impose stress on the shaft bearings.

12

which exhaust steam from high-pressure cylinders was used again in low-pressure cylinders of a larger size.

Model steam engines usually operate at pressures of between 0.703 and 5.625 kg/sq cm (10 and 80 psi), and sometimes more. Essential boiler fittings are gauges to monitor the water levels and steam pressures, and safety valves to ensure that the normal working pressures of the boilers are not exceeded. The larger models are usually equipped with at least two independent means for feeding water to the boiler whilst in steam; mechanical or hand pumps and live steam injectors are the most common methods used.

Liquid, gas and solid fuels can be used to raise steam, and model engines can also be operated by compressed air or turned by electric motors.

An advertising illustration from about 1901 of a Kingscote double-expansion compound marine engine with reversing gear.

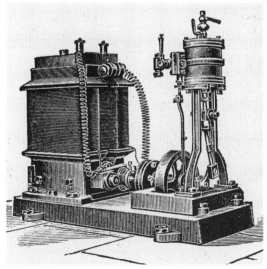

An advertising illustration from about 1905 of a British Engineering and Electrical Company direct-coupled generating set model with an inverted vertical single-cylinder engine.

13

A fine model of a horizontal mill engine, of about 1880. It is fitted with a Porter governor, multiple lubricator and eccentric-driven feed pump. Water storage and condensate tanks are located on the lower floor.

PROBLEMS AND PRACTICALITIES

At the beginning of the eighteenth century, when the first full-sized steam engines or 'fire-engines' were being built, one of the most formidable problems facing the early pioneers when constructing models or full-sized engines was the complete absence of machine tools. In 1500, long before steam engines were invented, Leonardo da Vinci had designed a number of machine tools, but none capable of producing engine parts to precise measurements was available when powerful steam engines were first developed.

As a result steam engines were being constructed before an engineering industry existed. As there were no mechanised workshops in which engine parts could be made accurately Thomas Savery set up his own workshop for the manufacture of steam engines in London, in 1702. The castings for many of the early machines were often made in local foundries, other parts being heated in on-site forges, wrought into shape on anvils and finished off with cold chisels, hammers, files, drills and other hand tools.

Each designer wrote his own specifications, even for screw thread sizes and pitches, and there were no recognised standards for the manufacture of engine parts. But the rapid increase in the use of steam power soon gave rise to serious maintenance and repair problems, and it became apparent that parts would have to be standardised so that they could be mass-produced. A need therefore arose for special machine tools to enable standardised, interchangeable engine parts to be made quickly, economically and accurately.

Although improved versions of the early water-powered cannon-boring machines, such as that evolved by Smeaton, were used to bore some small cylinders on the first steam engines, it was not until about 1775 that the first machine tool for the accurate boring of large cylinders was patented by John Wilkinson. It was the high standard of accuracy of this machine that enabled James Watt to build his improved steam engines.

Another machine tool of vital importance to engine builders was the lathe. As early as the fifteenth century small lathes

A catalogue illustration (about 1906) of a Stuart-Avery direct-coupled electrical generating set model with an inverted vertical engine.

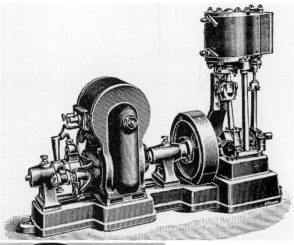

A horizontal mill-type model engine made from castings and parts supplied by W. Stevens's Model Dockyard, about 1900.

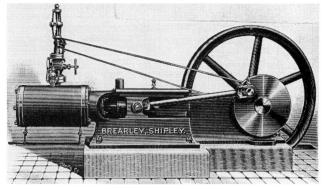

A pleasing model of a mill engine with disc crank and ball-type governor, made from castings and parts supplied by Brearley and Stevenson, about 1900.

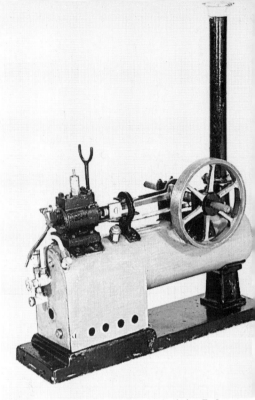

ABOVE LEFT: *A complete Marshall coal-fired steam set with horizontal engine built by F. I. Baines of Gainsborough in 1890.*
ABOVE RIGHT: *A simple overtype model engine with loco-type boiler and the safety valve on top of the steam chest. These semi-portable engines were used where space was limited or where the need for power was temporary.*
OPPOSITE ABOVE: *A horizontal steam plant with gas-fired marine-type, centre-flue boiler with cross tubes and two mill engines. The model is fitted with displacement-type lubricators, hand feed pump and a condensate tank.*
OPPOSITE BELOW LEFT: *A novelty centre-pillar model beam engine.*
OPPOSITE BELOW RIGHT: *A model horizontal mill engine with a Gurney-type coal-fired water tube boiler and steam blower valve, adjustable pillar-type safety valve, water gauge glass and hand-operated water feed pump.*

had been used for metalwork by clock-makers, who played a significant role in their development, and in particular of the ornamental lathes used mainly to produce line patterns. However, it was Henry Maudslay who, in 1798, converted the crude lathe into a precision machine tool for engineers by developing his revolutionary screw-cutting lathe.

Twenty years or so later Maudslay made some special machines for the mass-production of wooden pulley blocks for the Royal Navy at Portsmouth. These machines were designed by Marc Isambard Brunel, who invented many mecha-

nical tools, and were an outstanding success. Special machines were also developed by Fox, Roberts, Whitworth and others for building steam engines, and in 1830 a planing machine, believed to be one of the first of its kind in the world, was installed in the Boulton and Watt works in Soho, Birmingham.

Despite these achievements British engineers were slow to adopt new methods of working, and it was the Americans who took the initiative in using and developing machine tools. Fortunately Joseph Whitworth visited America and was greatly impressed by the progress

being made there in mechanising production methods. He became one of Britain's most notable advocates of machine tools and by 1833 had set up in business in Manchester as a toolmaker.

Because machine tools were not readily available many manufacturers had to design and make their own specialised machinery. A wide variety of machine tools were developed in this way, ranging from drilling machines to drop hammers. In the 1851 Great Exhibition in Hyde Park all the latest developments were displayed including those of Joseph Whitworth, whose tools had by that time gained a reputation for high quality. He became one of the most dominant toolmakers and was so aware of the importance of technology that he founded thirty Whitworth Scholarships. Sir Joseph Whitworth, as he became in 1869, is, however, best remembered for introducing standard *Whitworth screw threads* in 1841.

The 1851 Great Exhibition demons-trated the value of machine tools, and their manufacture expanded rapidly. Following the inauguration of public supplies of electricity in the 1880s, the machine-tool industry received a further boost with the introduction of electrical power drives.

Although by the middle of the nineteenth century the machine tool position had vastly improved for the makers of full-sized steam engines, no such tools had become available at a reasonable price for amateur constructors. Model engineering as a popular hobby was non-existent, and most of the model making was carried out by professionals.

If amateurs had the urge to make models in those early days they had many problems to overcome. Materials were expensive, and almost nothing had been done to cater for their needs. Few if any publications provided detailed plans or instructions for them, and they had mostly to start from scratch and build the entire model themselves, often without

An undertype engine with loco-type boiler built by B. Asher in 1903. This model has a reversing lever and is fitted with two different types of spring-loaded safety valves. Engines of this kind were popular during the second half of the nineteenth century.

using machine tools of any kind. For these reasons those who became model makers were often apprentices, who made models as part of their training, or sons of engineers or mechanics who learnt the necessary skills from their fathers.

Despite all the difficulties involved the desire to reproduce things in miniature has always been irresistible to creative people. Consequently, despite the problems, some amateurs were determined to make model steam engines. The whole business of amateur model making was, however, a long and arduous spare-time process and one had to be a real enthusiast to take it up. To start with the conditions of working were much worse than those which model makers have to contend with today. There were no electric heaters in the workshops and no fluorescent lights to work under. Instead a bogey-stove for heating might have been used in the winter, while flickering gas jets, smelly oil lamps or even feeble candlelights were often the only means of illumination under which delicate precision work had to be carried out. At the time scale model work was very exacting. It involved carrying out complex engineering operations and making items such as crankshafts and crossheads without the use of machine tools. Small lathes for home use were not marketed in the early days of model making, and even when they did become available the first ones were mostly worked by foot-

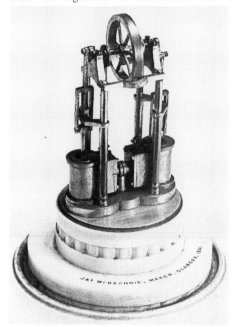

ABOVE: *A tiny four-pillar twin-cylinder vertical engine, on an ivory base and only 63 mm (2½ inches) high. This was made by James McKechnie of Glasgow in 1861.*

RIGHT: *This tiny scale working model of a beam engine weighs only 28.35 grams (1 ounce). It was made about 1846.*

treadles.

The use of lathes eventually revolutionised the work of model engineers by providing the means for turning, drilling, screw-cutting, buffing, polishing, grinding and many other operations. Without such facilities all these processes had to be dealt with by hand, including the making of taps and dies for the threading of nuts and bolts. Slotting work, which is now done on milling machines, was also laboriously carried out with hand tools.

The early amateur model makers also had to learn the hard way that exact scale modelling was not always a practical proposition, especially for working models. For example, if safety valves were made to an exact scale size they might be too small to protect the boilers. Similarly, the inside diameter of tiny water-gauge glasses could become so small that they would be of no practical use in indicating the water level. Scale-sized water tubes could sometimes restrict circulation instead of promoting it. All these practical problems and many more were well known to professional engineers. They must, however, have caused a lot of anxiety to the early amateur modellers, many of whom had to find out about the limitations of exact scale by trial and error.

The lot of the pioneer amateur model makers was not an easy one; only the most dedicated would have chosen to devote their spare time over many years to the hard and often difficult job of building good-quality scale models. That so many did is a measure of their determination and perseverance, and the excellence of the lovely models they created is a tribute to their engineering skills.

A contemporary model of a single-cylinder, two-pillar, rotative beam engine, built by Monsieur Bridoux of Pouilly in 1862. The valves operate from an eccentric on a lateral gear-driven shaft which also drives a Watt-type governor. Details include pierced brass latticework suspension links, decorative base and flywheel, turned columns and gold leaf scrollwork.

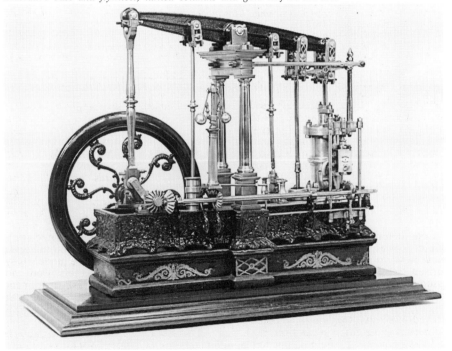

LEFT: *One of the earliest direct-acting engines was the table engine and for half a century it was used extensively for driving workshop machines. This model table engine in Gothic form is of historic importance, having been built by Richard Trevithick in 1803.*

RIGHT: *A model of a twin-cylinder, vertical pendulus engine, built by Maudslay in 1812, in which the cylinders are pivoted below the crankshaft, the piston rods being connected directly to the cranks. This enables the cylinders to swing to and fro as the flywheel revolves, thus lowering the total height of the engine.*

PIONEERS OF MODEL ENGINEERING

In engineering, experimental models were originally made before the full-scale machines were constructed. The reason for this was that it was much easier, cheaper and safer to use models to test the feasibility of ideas about steam power than to construct expensive full-sized engines which might not work at all. This practice marked the beginning of the science of industrial development modelling.

Long before model making became a hobby it was part of a major artistic movement in which the role of minia-turised replicas of industrial objects assumed great importance. Not only were models important as historical records of industrial development but, once having proved successful, they were then used as samples for the sales promotion of the full-sized machines. The construction of

working models also played a valuable part in the training of young craftsmen and engineers. Demonstration models were used to show how the steam engines worked, and a demand arose for models for display in factories and museums and for use as trophies and publicity emblems.

The real pioneers of model engineering were, therefore, the designers, builders and developers of the first steam machines, who all experimented with models before embarking upon full-scale construction. Some of these models they built themselves and others were no doubt made for them by instrument makers and opticians who were both equipped to carry out precision work with metals and skilled in doing so.

Thomas Savery was the first to patent a steam pump, and as early as 1699 a

A fine precision-built model of a horizontal mill engine by C. J. Coates, about 1898. It has a cut-away section on the cylinder to show the working of the piston. This engine is fitted with Corliss valves which give close speed control and also economy of operation.

working model of this atmospheric device was demonstrated to the Royal Society. Thomas Newcomen installed the first practical steam machine about 1712, but before that he had spent many years experimenting with models.

It was the unsatisfactory working of a model of a Newcomen atmospheric beam engine belonging to the University of Glasgow that first aroused the interest of James Watt in steam engines. This model was repaired by Watt about 1764, and he constructed a model of it to experiment with. Within the next two years he discovered why it ran out of steam so quickly and he invented the separate condenser, a most important advance in steam engine development. In his efforts to improve the design and efficiency of steam engines Watt made many models for experimental purposes. The first, of a separate condenser, has fortunately survived and is now preserved at the Science Museum in South Kensington, London.

A rare working model of a single-acting Uniflow engine with a cam-operated inlet valve, exhausting via a ring of tiny ports in the cylinder wall. At 4.219 kg/sq cm (60 psi) it turns at 2500 rpm and sounds like a machine gun.

The other famous model of Newcomen's engine which Watt repaired is preserved in the Hunterian Museum at the University of Glasgow.

James Nasmyth (1808-90), inventor of the steam-hammer, was a skilled model engineer and at one time made and sold model steam engines. One of the first amateur model engineers was John Smeaton (1724-92), who designed the first Eddystone Lighthouse to be built of stone. After studying a Newcomen engine, he built a model of it in 1765 and made extensive use of models in his experiments with steam engines.

At that time few amateurs had the multiple engineering skills needed for model making and, as previously indicated, most of the early models were made by professionals. However, during the second half of the nineteenth century amateur enthusiasts gradually began building model steam engines. During the latter part of the nineteenth and first part of the twentieth century many model makers became well known for the excellence of their work. They included Alfred Chadburn, the Coates brothers, E. W. Twining, Dr Bradbury Winter and H. J. Wood. By that time there were many other superb model makers.

Commercial organisations were quick to recognise the demand which would arise from model engineers for castings and parts, and a large number of firms were established to cater for their needs. Among them were such well known names as Batemans, the Clyde Model Dockyard, Stevens's Model Dockyard and Whitneys. The provision of materials and parts for models made it much easier for amateurs to take up model making, and the scene was thus set for the more widespread reproduction of prototype steam engines in miniature.

The vast possibilities of model engineering as a healthy means of self expression, as well as an interesting and educational hobby, had already been recognised and some articles about it appeared in the *Boy's Own Paper*. The first journal to make a serious attempt to promote interest in model engineering, in 1896, was *English Mechanics*. Two years later Percival Marshall, an engineer, published *The Model Engineer and Amateur Electrician*, a monthly magazine for amateur engineers. Less than a year later he formed, with some other model makers, the Society of Model Engineers, its

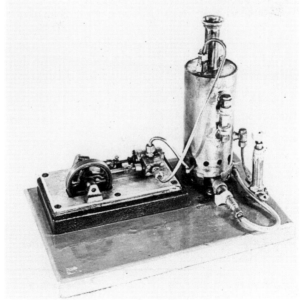

A small model horizontal engine with a gas-fired vertical centre-flue boiler complete with feed pump, safety valve and water gauge glass.

Front cover advertisement for 'The Model Engineer and Electrician' dated Thursday, 8th June, 1905.

object being the furtherance of the interests of amateur model makers. In 1910 the name was changed to the Society of Model and Experimental Engineers. With the publication of a specialist magazine for model makers and the foundation of a society that linked them together, the creative art of model engineering became popular throughout the world. In 1903 the magazine became a weekly one and the *Model Engineer*, as it is now called, is still published twice a month.

Two of the most notable of the designers who originally contributed articles to the magazine were Henry Greenly and Lillian Lawrence. Greenly was one of a small group of steam enthusiasts who, at the start of the twentieth century, took a leading part in the promotion of model engineering. He acted as a consultant to such firms as Bassett-Lowke, Stuart Turner and W. H. Jubb and, in addition to

his consultancy and design work on locomotives and railways, also designed some steam engines. Lawrence, who used the initials 'LBSC', was a great advocate of miniature engines (he disliked the term model). An engineman of the former London, Brighton and South Coast Railway, he contributed regularly from 1924 until 1959, and again in 1966 until his death the following year. He designed some simple stationary steam engines, but his speciality was the design and construction of miniature live-steam locomotives. Not only was he an experienced craftsman, but he had the gift of being able to impart information to others in a simple, friendly, down-to-earth style of instruction.

In 1899 another event had occurred which was to have a profound impact on model engineering: the setting up of a business by Wenman J. Bassett-Lowke to manufacture model steam engines and locomotives, and to produce castings and parts for the home construction of steam models by amateur engineers. At first Bassett-Lowke ran his business from his father's boiler-making and engineering firm in Northampton, but in 1908 he opened a shop at 257 High Holborn, London. Two years later he moved to number 112, which became famous as a showroom for high-class model engines. Other shops were later opened in Edinburgh and Manchester.

Although ornate and complicated lathes had been supplied by Holtzapffel and others as early as 1815 for home use by wealthy dilettantes, these were far too expensive for most amateurs. By the end of the nineteenth century, however, a number of ordinary lathes suitable for model engineers became available and in 1908 the Drummond Company of Guildford introduced their famous 101 mm (4 inch) centre round-bed lathe. This was specially designed for amateurs and at only £5 was excellent value. It was an instant success and continued in production for about twenty-eight years.

The model engineering movement was now well underway and another engineer who joined it, in 1906, was Stuart Turner. Some five or six years earlier he had

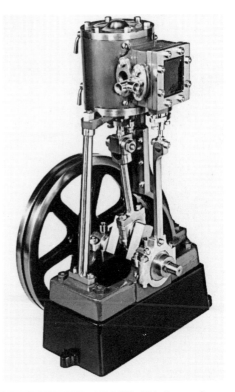

ABOVE: *This famous Stuart number 1 vertical engine was designed by Stuart Turner at the start of the twentieth century and is still in production. It is a beautifully proportioned model and castings and parts are still available.*

LEFT: *A stone crushing and grading plant model of about 1920, with a vertical coal-fired boiler, single-cylinder vertical engine and Stevenson's reversing link gear.*

designed and built his first model steam engine and Percival Marshall had encouraged him to make this and other engines available to model engineers in the form of castings and parts. He therefore set up in business to manufacture a range of models, and to supply these complete or in kits of parts for completion and assembly by home constructors. Over the years the firm's business expanded to cover models for museums and many full-sized engineering products. In the 1920s it claimed 'We make lighting plants for the country mansion or the doll's house'.

The genius of Percival Marshall was again expressed in 1907 when he founded the Model Engineer Exhibition in which model engineers could compete for prizes or simply display samples of their craftsmanship. The Exhibition continued to be held in London, mainly at the Agricultural and Horticultural and Seymour halls until 1977, when it was transferred to the Wembley Conference Centre. Later venues have varied.

The early pioneers, as well as creating a splendid peace-time hobby, also developed the model engineering skills which proved of enormous value in wartime. Models were then urgently needed for military and naval projects such as the Mulberry Harbour installations, the models for which were made by Bassett-Lowke Limited.

The author with Miss O'Connor of 'Steam Age' examining a model in the corner of the original shop in Cadogan Street, London.

26

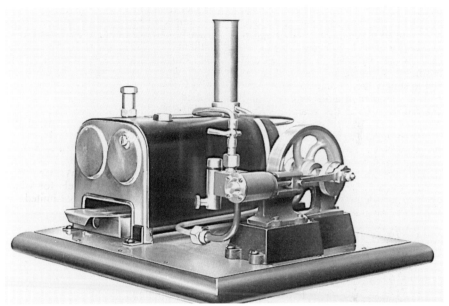

An elegant Bassett-Lowke model steam set with a Tangye engine made by Bassett-Lowke, and a Stuart Turner twin-drum horizontal boiler with vaporising-type spirit lamp (about 1955).

MODEL ENGINEERING FIRMS

From the end of the eighteenth century onwards, specialist firms were set up to cater for the needs of model engineers and to supply finished models. It is impossible to list them all in this book but those given below are some of the earlier and better known firms.

J. Bateman and Company, London. About 1774 to 1890. An old-established firm, with a model shop in High Holborn, which made good quality brass components for the home construction of model steam engines and locomotives. The company claimed to have the largest selection of working models in the world.

Bassett-Lowke Limited, Northampton. About 1899 to present. Bassett-Lowke was one of the foremost pioneers of scale modelling and he was famed for the excellence of his annual catalogue, the first of which was published in 1901, the last in June 1963. After Bassett-Lowke's death in 1953, the Northampton factory concentrated on building models for

museums and industry, and the manufacture of model steam engines, locomotives, castings and so on was run down. Subsequently, in 1965, their famous showrooms in London and Manchester were sold to Beatties, and a notable era in the history of steam models was closed.

Although the production of a standard range of models ceased, the making of all types of models could still be obtained by special order. Moreover, in 1968 a new company, Bassett-Lowke (Railways) Limited, was set up with its retail headquarters at the internationally famous 'Steam Age' shop at 59 Cadogan Street, London. A limited range of fine quality steam locomotives and other models were still being manufactured then for connoisseurs while 'Steam Age' also sold second-hand steam engines and locomotives together with castings and parts for model engineers. After moving to 19 Abingdon Road, Kensington, for a short time, 'Steam Age' was, alas, closed.

Bond's O' Euston Road Limited, London. About 1887. This well-known firm specialised in the supply of castings and parts for the home construction of steam locomotives. In the early years some model stationary and marine engines were also sold, and later on sets of castings for their Bonzone mill engine were supplied. In 1929 Mr Arthur W. Bond, the founder, retired from the business and was succeeded by Mr S. D. Phillips. The business was transferred from 357 Euston Road, London, to Midhurst, Sussex, in 1974, and catered for model makers on a reduced scale.

Alfred Chadburn, Sheffield. About 1820s to 1880s. Alfred Chadburn was one of the Chadburn Brothers who were 'Optical, Mathematical, and Philosophical Instrument Makers', of Sheffield and Liverpool. As well as being an optician he was a great model maker who, with the use of a lot of brass and decorative work, made intricate models of steam engines and locomotives.

Clyde Model Dockyard, Glasgow. About 1789 to 1930s. An old-established firm which originally started as model makers to the Admiralty and later extended its business to include models of stationary and marine

steam engines, steam locomotives and hot-air engines, etc.

Kingscote Brothers and Williams, Manchester. Established about 1901. This firm made high-class models of steam engines and specialised in constructing model electric light plants.

R. A. Lee and Company, London. Established about 1880. This well known model firm advertised in the 1880s as 'Makers of Steam Engines' and was famed for its brass castings.

Lucas and Davies, London. Established about 1868. Another well known firm that sold finished models of steam engines and boilers, and supplied sets of castings. Model locomotives were also made.

Stevens's Model Dockyard, London. About 1843 to 1930. One of the most famous British companies, it was established for the purpose of 'encouraging the rising generation, amateur mechanics etc, in scientific research, mechanical recreations and instructive amusements'. A wide range of steam models was supplied, also castings and components.

J. Sutcliffe and Company, Leek. About 1882

to 1920s. One of the smaller firms, it was set up primarily for the manufacture of castings and components for model makers. Complete models were also sold. It changed its name to the Leek Model Company, and by 1905 it was advertising as the British Engineering and Electrical Company.

Stuart Turner Limited, Henley-on-Thames. About 1906 to present. The origins of this renowned firm stem from a small vertical steam engine which Mr Turner designed at the beginning of the twentieth century and which is still in production. Having started his engineering business as a part-time hobby, Stuart Turner gave his full time to the development of the firm in 1906 and a limited company was formed. He eventually left the business in 1920 and died shortly before his seventieth birthday in 1938.

An innovation of this progressive company was the launching in 1971 of the Stuart International Model Engineers Club. Known as SIMEC, this club ceased to operate in the 1980s. In 1991 Stuart Models underwent a change of ownership, with the production and sales departments moving to Guernsey, where a large selection of the Stuart models range is displayed. Under the new ownership of Jones & Bradburn the excellence of standards and quality associated with the Stuart models name is being commendably maintained.

E. W. Twining Models Limited, Northampton. Established about 1909. Mr Twining was a well known professional engineer who built splendid scale models to high standards. He specialised in exhibition work, and especially in the construction of steam locomotives.

Whitney, London. About 1877 to the 1940s. This old-established firm supplied high-class marine-type model steam engines and water motors.

W. J. Wood, London. Established about 1860. Mr Wood, the father of the famous conductor, Sir Henry Wood, was an instrument maker and professional model engineer. He made some superb steam engines and also cranes, fire engines and steam locomotives.

A Stuart number 10H horizontal engine made from castings and parts. This powerful model, suitable for driving a dynamo, was made about 1950, and is still available.

A model of a Porter Allen high-speed direct-coupled electrical generating set.

CONCLUSION

Model steam engines, which all the early pioneers did so much to promote, are miniature works of art having both intrinsic and aesthetic value. Many early models were made to such high standards of technical excellence and artistic beauty that discerning connoisseurs now equate our Victorian miniature engineering heritage with other great art forms throughout the world, a recognition it richly deserves.

Originally model engineering was regarded as an exclusively male occupation, but nowadays superb prize-winning mod-els are being made by women as well as men. In this age of instant pleasure and excitement, why is it that people are prepared to spend so much time and effort in constructing complex scale models? Only those who have experienced the sheer joy and satisfaction of creative modelling can fully answer this question. But the exquisite miniature engines the enthusiasts produce certainly reflect something of the love, pride and skill of their creators; they will also ensure that the massive prototypes they portray will never be forgotten.

FURTHER READING

Ball, Eric E. *100 Years of Model Engineering, 1898-1998*. SM&EE, 1997.
Bradley, Ian. *A History of Machine Tools*. Model and Allied Publications, 1972.
Catalogue of Stuart Models. Stuart Models, Guernsey, 1998.
Engineering in Miniature (magazine). TEE Publishing.
Evans, Martin. *Model Engineering*. Pitman, 1977.
Hadlow, H. R. *Introducing Model Engineering*. Percival Marshall, 1947. (Out of print.)
Harris, K. N. *Model Stationary and Marine Steam Engines*. Model and Allied Publications, 1958.
Hasluck, Paul N. *The Model Engineer's Handybook*. Crosby, Lockwood & Son, 1888. Reprinted by TEE Publishing.
Law, R. J. *The Steam Engine*. HMSO, 1965.
Model Engineer (magazine). Nexus Media Ltd.
Muncaster, H. *Model Stationary Engines*, 1912. Reprinted by TEE Publishing, 1979.
Rolt, L. T. C. *Tools for the Job*. B. T. Batsford, 1965.
Thomas, George. *Model Engineers Workshop Manual*. TEE Publishing.

'Old crocks' being lovingly restored in a workshop.

PLACES TO VISIT

Museum displays may be altered and readers are advised to telephone before visiting to check that relevant items are on show, as well as to find out the opening times.

Blackpool Mill and Caverns, Canaston Bridge, Narberth, Pembrokeshire. Telephone: 01437 541233.

Bressingham Steam Museum and Gardens, Bressingham, Diss, Norfolk IP22 2AB. Telephone: 01379 687386.

British Engineerium, Nevill Road, Hove, East Sussex BN3 7QA. Telephone: 01273 559583.

Discovery Museum, Blandford Square, Newcastle upon Tyne NE1 4JA. Telephone: 0191-232 6789.

Kew Bridge Steam Museum, Green Dragon Lane, Brentford, Middlesex TW8 0EN. Telephone: 0181-568 4757.

Leeds Industrial Museum, Armley Mills, Canal Road, Armley, Leeds LS12 2QF. Telephone: 01132 637861.

Levens Hall Steam Collection, Levens Hall, Kendal, Cumbria LA8 0PD. Telephone: 015395 60321.

The Museum of Science and Industry in Manchester, Liverpool Road, Castlefield, Manchester M3 4FP. Telephone: 0161-832 2244.

Poldark Mine and Heritage Centre, Poldark Mine, Wendron, Helston, Cornwall TR13 0ER. Telephone: 01326 563166.

Science Museum, Exhibition Road, South Kensington, London SW7 2DD. Telephone: 0171-938 8000.

The International Model Show is held annually in London in association with the SM&EE. This show will be best known to many under its old title of the Model Engineer Exhibition.

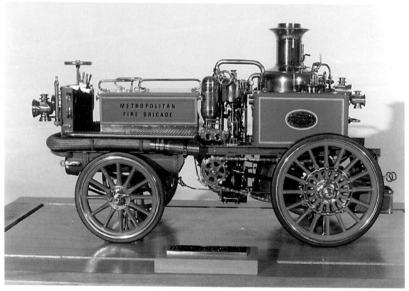

A Merryweather self-propelled fire engine, c.1905; a one-sixteenth scale model made by Mrs Cherry Hill.

32